ABRSM
PUBLISHING

The Associated Boar
the Royal Schools of

GU01033166

Theory of
Music Exams

MODEL ANSWERS

GRADE 5

2007

Welcome to ABRSM's *Theory of Music Exams Model Answers*, Grade 5, 2007. These answers are a useful resource for pupils and teachers preparing for ABRSM theory exams and should be used alongside the relevant published theory exam papers.

All the answers in this booklet would receive full marks but not all possible answers have been included for practicable reasons. In these cases other reasonable alternatives may also be awarded full marks. For composition-style questions (where candidates must complete a rhythm, compose a melody based on a given opening or set text to music) only one example of the many possible answers is given.

For more information on how theory papers are marked and some general advice on taking theory exams, please refer to the booklet *These Music Exams* by Clara Taylor, which is available free of charge and can be downloaded from www.abrsm.org.

Using these answers

- Answers are given in the same order and, where possible, in the same layout as in the exam papers, making it easy to match answer to question.

- Where it is necessary to show the answer on a stave, the original stave is printed in grey with the answer shown in black, for example:

- Alternative answers are separated by an oblique stroke (/) or by *or*, for example:

  getting slower / gradually getting slower

- Answers that require the candidate to write out a scale or chord have been shown at one octave only. Reasonable alternatives at different octaves can also receive full marks.

Theory Paper Grade 5 2007 A
Model Answers

1 (a) (i) comfortably / conveniently (2)

    (ii) (2)

    (iii) (3)

  (b) 1: diminished 7th (8)
     2: augmented 4th
     3: compound major 3rd / major 10th
     4: minor 6th

2 (10)

etc.

3 (a) (i) slow / at ease / leisurely (2)
        semi-staccato / slightly detached / slightly separated (2)
        repeat the passage from the beginning (2)
   (ii) turn / upper turn (2)
   (iii) appoggiatura / leaning note (2)

  (b) (i) Chord A: V 3rd / V b (2)
       Chord B: IV root / IV a (2)

   (ii) Ic   –   V (2)
      or $\frac{6}{4}$ – $\frac{5}{3}$

   (iii) (4)

(c) (i)   (2)

(ii) subdominant   (2)

(iii)   Instrument: violin / viola   Family: strings   (4)
     or   Instrument: flute / oboe / clarinet   Family: woodwind
     or   Instrument: trumpet   Family: brass

(iv) transposing   /   non-transposing   (2)
     (if answer to 3 (c) (iii) was   *(if answer to 3 (c) (iii) was*
     clarinet or trumpet)   *violin, viola, flute or oboe)*

4   (10)

(a)

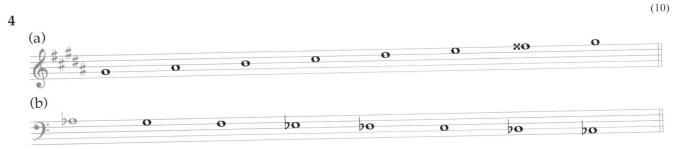

(b)

5   (10)

6   *There are many ways of completing this question. Either of the specimen completions below would receive full marks.* (15)

EITHER

(a)   bassoon

OR

(b)

Blows   the   wind — to - day,   And   the   sun   and the   rain — are

fly - ing.

4

7 EITHER

  (a) Chord A: II / A minor   Chord C: IV / C major   (10)

          Chord B: V / D major   Chord D: V / D major

                                                      Chord E: I / G major

OR

(b)

Theory Paper Grade 5   2007   B
Model Answers

1 (a) (i) Bar 1: $\frac{7}{8}$ (4)

               Bar 2: $\frac{5}{8}$

      (ii)   three quavers in the time of two quavers / three eighth-notes in the time of two   (2)
             eighth-notes / three quavers in the time of one crotchet / three eighth-notes
             in the time of one quarter-note

      (iii)   (3)

  (b) (i)   (4)

      (ii)   F♯ minor
                                             (2)

2 1:   diminished 7th
    2:    perfect 11th / compound perfect 4th   (10)
    3:    major 6th
    4:    augmented 5th
    5:    minor 3rd

3

Rachmaninoff, Piano Concerto in D minor, Op. 30 (transposed)

4 (a) (i) rather slowly / slightly slow / a little slowly   (2)
heavy / heavily   (2)
72 crotchets in a minute / 72 quarter-notes in a minute   (2)

    (ii) simple   (2)
triple

    (iii) 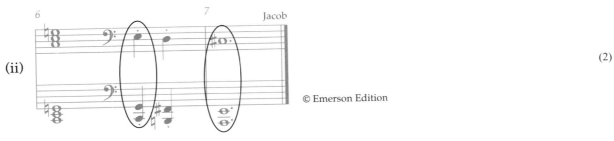   (2)

(b) (i) Triad A: A minor   Triad B: C minor   Triad C: B♭ minor   (6)

    (ii)   (2)

© Emerson Edition

    (iii) F / F♮ / F natural   (2)

(c) (i)   (2)

    (ii) false   (2)
true   (2)

    (iii)   Family: string   Instrument: double bass   (4)
     or   Family: brass   Instrument: tuba / bass tuba

(10)

5 (a)

(b)

6 *There are many ways of completing this question. Either of the specimen completions below would receive full marks.* (15)

EITHER

(a) trumpet

OR

(b)

I love to rise in a sum - mer morn When the birds ____ sing ___ on

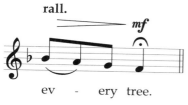

ev - ery tree.

7 EITHER

(a) Chord A: II / D minor   Chord D: IV / F major
    Chord B: I / C major   Chord E: I / C major
    Chord C: V / G major

(10)

OR

(b)

Theory Paper Grade 5   2007   C
Model Answers

1 (a) (i) Bar 2: $\frac{5}{4}$ (4)

           Bar 3: $\frac{3}{4}$

       (ii)   suddenly   (2)

(b) (i)   (5)

       (ii)   compound   (2)
               quadruple

       (iii)   (2)

2   1:   diminished 5th   (10)
     2:    augmented 2nd
     3:    perfect 4th
     4:    minor 7th
     5:    major 14th / compound major 7th

3   (10)

Dunhill, Phantasy Suite (transposed)

© Copyright Boosey & Hawkes Music Publishers Ltd
Reproduced by permission.

4 (a) (i)   lively but tenderly / lively but delicately   (5)
               light / nimble   (2)

       (ii)   (3)

(b) (i)   Chord Y: IV 3rd / IV b   (2)
            Chord Z: V root / V a   (2)

       (ii)   (2)

(iii) .... (2)

(iv) E minor

(2)

(c) (i) Bass   Baritone   Tenor   Contralto   Soprano   (4)

    (ii) brass   (2)

        bassoon   (2)

        viola   (2)

5

(a)   (10)

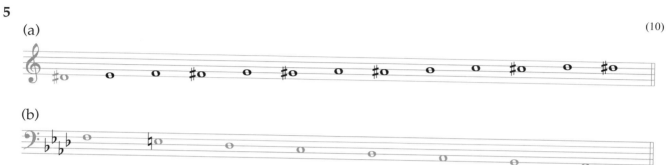

(b)

6 *There are many ways of completing this question. Either of the specimen completions below would receive full marks.* (15)

EITHER

(a) violin

Andante

OR

(b)

Moderato

Fall,   leaves,   fall;   die, flowers, a-way;   Length - en night ____ and

shor - ten day.

7 EITHER

(a) Chord A: IV / B♭ major   Chord C: II / G minor
     Chord B: I / F major   Chord D: V / C major
                                           Chord E: I / F major

OR

(b)

Theory Paper Grade 5 2007 S
Model Answers

1 (a)   1:   minor 9th / compound minor 2nd   (8)
          2:     augmented 3rd
          3:     major 6th
          4:     diminished 4th

    (b) (i)   Chord A: V 3rd / V b   (2)
               Chord B: I 5th / I c   (2)

        (ii)

(3)

2

The tenor part could also be written using the following clef:

Full marks would also be awarded if the alto and tenor parts were given in the alto and tenor clefs:

3 (a) (i)   fairly quick / quite quick / not quite as quick as Allegro   (2)
            72 dotted crotchets in a minute / 72 dotted quarter-notes in a minute /   (2)
                72 dotted crotchet beats in a minute / 72 dotted quarter-note beats in a minute
            forced / accented   (2)
            repeat the passage from the beginning   (2)

    (ii) acciaccatura / grace note / crushed note   (2)

  (b) (i)    (4)

    (ii) F major   (2)
          D major   (2)

    (iii) compound   (2)
          duple

  (c) (i)   <u>oboe</u>   (4)
          woodwind

    (ii) false   (2)
          true   (2)
          true   (2)

4   (10)
  (a)

  (b)

5   (10)

6 *There are many ways of completing this question. Either of the specimen completions below would receive full marks.* (15)

EITHER

(a)　flute

OR

(b)

The snow came fly - ing, In __ large __ white flakes, 　　fall - ing

on _____ the ci - ty brown.

7 **EITHER** (10)

(a)　Chord A:　II / D minor　　　　　Chord D:　IV / F major
　　　Chord B:　V / G major　　　　　Chord E:　I / C major
　　　Chord C:　I / C major

OR

(b)

ABRSM PUBLISHING

The Associated Board of the Royal
Schools of Music (Publishing) Limited
24 Portland Place, London W1B 1LU
United Kingdom
www.abrsmpublishing.com